THE INAUGURAL ADDRESSES OF AMERICAN PRESIDENTS

The Public Philosophy and Rhetoric

Dante Germino

With a Preface and Introduction by

Kenneth W. Thompson

UNIVERSITY
PRESS OF
AMERICA

LANHAM • NEW YORK • LONDON

THE INAUGURAL ADDRESSES OF AMERICAN PRESIDENTS

THE PUBLIC PHILOSOPHY AND RHETORIC

VOLUME VII IN A SERIES
FUNDED BY THE
JOHN and MARY R. MARKLE FOUNDATION

All University Press of America books are produced on acid-free
paper which exceeds the minimum standards set by the National
Historical Publications and Records Commission.

THE INAUGURAL ADDRESSES OF AMERICAN PRESIDENTS:

THE PUBLIC PHILOSOPHY AND RHETORIC

TABLE OF CONTENTS

PREFACE

by

Kenneth W. Thompson

In the autumn of 1980, the Miller Center of Public Affairs published a widely discussed report on presidential press conferences which carried the imprimatur of a distinguished national commission co-chaired by Governor Linwood Holton and Ray Scherer. In the winter of 1981, James Brady in introducing President Reagan's first press conference announced that the Reagan administration would follow the recommendations of the Miller Center commission. These included a requirement that reporters wishing to ask questions raise their hands and be recognized by the President so that the circus atmosphere of the questioning might be replaced by some reasonable measure of decorum. The commission also called for greater regularity in the holding of press conferences, a practice which has not been fully observed by the Reagan administration any more than it was by its immediate predecessors.

In the discussions of the Miller Center Commission on the Presidential Press Conference, members and witnesses who testified commented on the breadth of the relations between Presidents and the press. We were warned repeatedly that presidential press conferences were but one arena in which such relations occurred. It was noted not by one but by numerous authorities that speeches, town meetings, receptions, or press or "photo opportunities," trips and celebrations all were the scene of interaction between the President, the press and the public. We were urged to cast our net more broadly than the press conference.

The purpose of the present study by Professor Dante Germino of the Woodrow Wilson Department of Government and Foreign Affairs at the University of Virginia is to examine one important sphere of presidential-press-public relations. It is surprising that so few studies have been made of inaugural addresses. They constitute the first presentation by an incoming President of himself and his program. For Presidents who are reelected, the inaugural address may also involve a report on four years or less of stewardship. As the first 100 days of an administration constitute a time when new legislation can most likely be passed, a President's new ideas and policies are more likely to be received with enthusiasm and warmth at the beginning rather than the end of his administration.

It would be false, however, to suggest that the role of inaugural addresses by Presidents is everywhere the same. The context of such addresses is the spirit of the times. While the President imposes himself upon the form of the address, it is the times in part that shape the President's outlook and what he feels called on to say. Moreover, each historical era brings with it social and intellectual tendencies that influence contemporary thought.

What Professor Germino, who is Virginia's foremost political theorist, asks his readers to do is to read and compare with him significant passages from representative inaugural addresses. That reading in and of itself would be a sufficient excuse for the study. However, Germino, as he proceeds, asks a series of penetrating questions about each inaugural, its assumptions and intent and the major direction of thought and philosophy of the President who was its author.

It will remain for future study, reflection and writing by this highly original political thinker to examine other closely related questions. What about the other presidential addresses including those to the world at the United Nations? What can be said about the formative or deforming influence of the comparatively new profession of presidential speech writers? Has television had an effect? If so, how can we measure it? To what extent do the peculiar strengths and weaknesses of individual Presidents affect perspectives on presidential addresses? Has the flight from history and philosophy influenced the character of inaugural addresses? What about changing public attitudes toward presidential rhetoric and rhetoric in general?

Professor Germino has not neglected questions such as these. However, those of greater generality fall outside the scope of this little volume. They are questions to which Germino has pledged himself to conduct further inquiry. Until the results of future studies are completed, the present study of inaugural addresses provides an important introduction to the central issues.

INTRODUCTION

by

Kenneth W. Thompson

The sub-title of Professor Germino's study is *The Public Philosophy and Rhetoric*. He has seen fit to consider presidential addresses in their broadest context. For this reason, his volume goes well beyond the technical and procedural issues of presidential-press relations fulfilling in this respect the charge laid on members of the original Miller Center Commission. It asks the questions "what" and "why" whereas earlier studies in the series had concentrated primarily on "how." If purpose and politics are inseparably connected, an englobing framework of thought is as important for topics of the presidency and the press as for any other sphere of politics.

It is worth taking note that in raising the question of public philosophy, Germino has taken a stand (and not for the first time) in opposition to certain prevailing views in political science. The drift in the discipline has been away from discussion of values. Leading scholars have prided themselves on the creation of a value-free science of politics and society. Whatever his other aims and goals in this essay, Germino has launched a direct attack on this approach.

For the founding fathers, it was inconceivable that politics not be viewed in relation to purpose. The fateful division between law and politics which has been especially destructive in recent American approaches to international politics was ruled out by the most respected thinkers. Thus Hamilton, Jefferson and Franklin all learned from Vattel and other European thinkers that the law of nations and the balance of power must be seen in their interrelationship, not as being mutually exclusive.

Only a few recent American writers have sought to revive interest in the public philosophy. Walter Lippmann stands in the forefront of this group. The rather critical response to his work which he saw as the climax of his intellectual journey attests to the general uneasiness of Americans when anyone addresses the subject. Similarly, Professor Hans J. Morgenthau expressed disappointment that his one book which evoked the least reaction of any kind was *The Purpose of American Politics*. Even those writers who seemingly are concerned with the underlying questions of a public philosophy seem to prefer dressing it in the garb of other concepts such as civil religion.

Yet the public philosophy for the founders was an outlook and approach far closer to the citizen and his government than ideas of pseudo-religion or political ideology. The great merit of Professor Germino's work is to bring our thinking back to its foundations in the public philosophy. It is the public philosophy that takes us back to the cardinal ideas of authority, the state, individualism, civic virtue and power. Because it throws the spotlight on the core of politics and governance, this perspective provides a superior framework for considering the relations of Presidents and the press. A narrower stress on skills and techniques would merely recapitulate what others have said, perhaps better than the theorist, about organizing and conducting press conferences.

We have moved in this series from quite specific concerns to the broad issues of the public philosophy. In this journey, the series has been guided and informed by the philosopher's principle of proceeding from the particular to the general. Thus we have undertaken to leave for those who may seek clarity in a complex sphere a series of studies that illuminate concrete questions of method and provide overall principles of philosophy that determine the main lines of presidential-press relations.

The "Public Philosophy" in the Rhetoric of American Presidents

Dante Germino*
University of Virginia

I. RHETORIC AND THE PUBLIC PHILOSOPHY

In the American political system, presidential speech commands exceptional attention from press and public. Such a fact is hardly to be attributed in the first instance to a particular president's skill in the art of delivery. While some presidents have been acclaimed first-class orators (Wilson, the Roosevelts, Kennedy and Reagan), most have either been regarded as indifferent speakers, or they have exhibited some idiosyncrasy which often spoiled the effect of their delivery. Thomas Jefferson was diffident on the podium. Abraham Lincoln was mocked in the press for the "poor delivery" of his Gettysburg Address. Jimmy Carter often looked tense and unhappy. Nixon looked—like Nixon. Gerald Ford seemed clumsy, as if he were always in danger of falling down. As for Lyndon Johnson, here is an account of a friendly biographer:

> Terrified of making slips swearing or using ungrammatical constructions, Johnson insisted on reading from formal texts. Facial muscles frozen in place, except for the simpering smile, he projected an image of feigned propriety, dullness, and dishonesty.[1]

* Grateful acknowledgement is made to the Miller Center for Public Affairs, University of Virginia, for a research grant on this project.

A denizen of the electronic age, Johnson insisted on speaking from a monstrous podium, which reporters nicknamed "mother" because it "encompassed the orating president with enormous sound-sensitive arms."[2] Addicted to this massive teleprompter, Johnson took it everywhere, and felt utterly lost if by chance it had been left in Washington.

As Wayne Booth has written, and as every faculty member knows, "the primary mental act of man is to assent to truth rather than to detect error," to "take in" and even "to be taken in" rather than to "resist being taken in."[3] That being the case, it is not difficult to understand why an American president has an enormous advantage over his opposition in the contest to persuade the electorate. As James Barber has said, the presidency

> is much more than an institution. It is a focus of feelings . . . [Unlike Congress] the presidency is the focus of the most intense and persistent emotions in the American polity. The President is a symbolic leader, the one figure who draws together the people's hopes and fears for the . . . future.[4]

How is it that the attention of the American public is focused on the rhetoric of presidents regardless of their deficiencies in technical skill at speech-making? One answer, of course, is that a president's policies affect one's pocketbook. My own reading of presidential speeches, however, convinces me that there is another, deeper reason: Americans, regardless of party, tend at crucial times to look to the President for hope and for a rearticulation of the nation's "public philosophy."[5]

It is primarily by expressing the "public philosophy" that American presidents engage in the practice of the "rhetoric of assent," which, again to quote Wayne Booth, is a kind of rhetoric aimed at "finding what really warrants assent because any reasonable person ought to be persuaded by what has been said."[6] In this context, the "reasonable person" is someone who has been schooled in the common creed of Americans.

That there is an American public philosophy, and that the United States is uniquely a society begun and held together by a body of beliefs typically expressed in propositional form, is now so firmly established as the premise of the most acute observers of the American scene as here to require no justification. American "exceptionalism" is the theme of significant studies by Alexis de Tocqueville, Werner Sombart, Gunnar Myrdal, Louis Hartz, and, most recently, Juergen Gebhardt. As Gebhardt has noted, the United States is held together by a "civil theology" *(theologia civilis)* developed during the period of the struggle for national independence. Following John

Adams, Gebhardt calls this civil theology, "Americanism."[7]

I have chosen to employ the more recent term "public philosophy" instead of the ancient term civil theology—or the modern concept of "civil religion"—in this study, because while every society has a civil theology—or minimal set of beliefs about man, society, and history—the United States has expanded such a minimal set of beliefs into a set of detailed propositions. At the same time, it has not embraced an ideology, or a set of all-encompassing principles for interpreting and guiding reality, as was the case in the USSR or Hitler's Germany. The public philosophy, although a more developed set of propositions than the Varronic civil theology, deliberately leaves space for private vision and insight.[8]

One need only compare the political cultures of the United States and Italy, for example, to observe in the latter a sedimentation over the ages of diverse regional histories, rigid class structures, and acute ideological conflicts. By comparison, the United States was created all at once through the enunciation of a set of propositions held to be "self-evident" to "reasonable persons." In the matchless eloquence of Thomas Jefferson's *Declaration of Independence:*

> We hold these truths to be self-evident: that all men are created equal, that they are endowed by their Creator with certain unalienable Rights, that among these are Life, Liberty, and the pursuit of Happiness.

Americans then are uniquely a propositional people, a people cemented together by a public philosophy. As Gunnar Myrdal has written, "America, compared to every other country in Western civilization . . .has the most explicitly expressed system of general ideas in reference to human interrelations."[9] "It is remarkable," Myrdal continues,

> that a vast democracy with so many cultural disparities has been able to reach this unanimity of ideals and to elevate them supremely over the threshold of popular perception. Totalitarian fascism and nazism have not succeeded in accomplishing a similar result in spite of the fact that those governments have used violence . . . .[10]

Even the most cursory examination of presidential speeches confirms the validity of Myrdal's observation. To quote at random from a recent address, Jimmy Carter's commencement address at the University of Notre Dame on May 22, 1977:

> In ancestry, religion, color, place of origin and cultural background, we Americans are as diverse a nation as the world has ever seen. No common mystique of blood or soil unites us. What draws us together . . . is a belief . . . .[11]

3

Or to quote from Lyndon Johnson's inaugural address:
Our destiny in the midst of change will rest on the unchanged
character of the American people and on their faith.[12]

Granted that such an American public philosophy exists, what is
its content beyond the general formulation given to it by Thomas
Jefferson? Inevitably upon this subject there is much controversy. In
a sense, the entire political debate in the United States has concerned the interpretation, application, and revision of the public
philosophy.

Myrdal, writing in the context of the post World War II struggle
to eliminate legally enforced segregation of whites and blacks in the
public schools and in public accommodations, especially in the
American South, understandably locates the core of the public
philosophy in the concept of equality. He contends that equality
"was given the supreme rank and the rights to liberty are posited as
derived from equality." He cites Jefferson's first draft of the *Declaration* as illustrative of its author's intent. In that draft Jefferson
declared that all men are created equal "and from that equal Creation they derive rights inherent and unalienable."[13]

Even if one were to grant Myrdal's thesis that equality takes pre-
cedence over liberty in the American public philosophy, one would
be left with the question "equality for what?" This question of
course has been a vexing one in the current efforts to reduce the ac-
cumulated effects of racial discrimination through "affirmative action," employment "goals" and the like. The Bakke case regarding
medical school admissions is a famous example of the difficulties of
interpreting the meaning of equality—and of "equal opportunity."

Rather than accept *a priori* any particular reading of the American public philosophy's content, I propose to examine how that philosophy has been interpreted in the rhetoric of presidents. While
there obviously are other sources for the American public philosophy, it is my contention that its authoritative articulation has occurred in the rhetoric of presidents and that, indeed, one of the prin-
cipal functions of the presidency is precisely to engage in this process. By this I do not mean to argue that the public philosophy is
what a given president says it is, simply because he says it. Indeed,
the public philosophy is something given in the culture which limits
the thinking of its political leaders and the terms and resolutions of
the political debate. For a president to be judged as "successful," he
must manage to persuade the public that he is acting within, and has
accurately read the *direction* for the country implicit in, the public
philosophy.

4

The presidential inaugural address offers a particularly fertile field for investigation. From the beginning, when George Washington instituted the practice, each president has made a speech immediately before or after taking the constitutionally prescribed oath of office. The inaugural addresses, therefore, lend themselves to comparison in a way which other presidential addresses do not. They are prepared with extreme care, for each president is conscious that his words are not only for his immediate audience but for "history" as well.

II. THE PUBLIC PHILOSOPHY IN THE INAUGURAL ADDRESSES OF PRESIDENTS[14]

When one has finished stripping away the conventional ceremonial utterances appropriate to the installation of a republic's head of state, one is left with a core of ideas noteworthy for their specificity. These ideas constitute the public philosophy of the American polity. Although there is development and change in these ideas as one moves through the decades, on the whole the continuity of political thought is remarkable.

In the first instance, the American public philosophy is theocentric or God-centered rather than anthropocentric, or man-centered in character. Although the form of reference to divine being is usually deistic, the background of the deistic language is clearly that of Judeo-Christian revelation. Thus, Washington offers his "fervent supplications to that Almighty Being who rules over the universe, who presides in the councils of nations, and whose providential aids can supply every human defect . . . ." (2) John Adams invokes the blessing of "that Being who is supreme over all, the Patron of Order, the Fountain of Justice, and the Protector in all ages of the world of virtuous liberty . . . ." (11) Thomas Jefferson venerates "an overruling Providence, which by all its dispensations proves that it delights in the happiness of man here and his greater happiness hereafter . . . ." (15) Andrew Jackson declares his "firm reliance on the goodness of that Power whose providence mercifully protected our national infancy . . . ." (57) James K. Polk asks that "Almighty Ruler of the Universe in whose hands are the destinies of nations and of men to guard this Heaven-favored land . . . ." (90). He refers to "Divine Being" (98) and "the wisdom of Omnipotence" (90). Zachary Taylor (101), Franklin Pierce (108, 109) and James Buchanan all have "Providence" as a central theme of their addresses. Abraham Lincoln counsels submission of both North and South to the "Almighty Ruler of Nations." (121) Ulysses S. Grant invokes the aid of the "Great Maker" (103), while Rutherford B. Hays refers to the "Divine Hand" (137, 140). Subsequent presidents refer to "Almighty God" (154, 179, 196), the "Supreme Being" (167), the "Lord Most High" (177), and the "Giver of Good" (184).

A theme closely associated with theocentricism in the inaugural addresses is *exceptionalism.* God has made of America his (new) "chosen country":

> No people can be bound to acknowledge and adore the Invisible Hand which conducts the affairs of men more than those of the United States. (2) [Washington, 1st inaugural].

> Kindly separated by nature . . . from the exterminating havoc of one quarter of the globe, . . . possessing a chosen country, with room enough for our descendents to the thousandth and thousandth generation . . . ." (15) [Jefferson, 1st inaugural].

> [Invoking] the favor of that Being in whose hands we are, who led our fathers, as Israel of old, from their native land and planted them in a country flowing with all the necessaries and comforts of life . . . . (21) [Jefferson, 2nd inaugural].

> [Prays to] that Almighty Being . . . who has kept us in His hands from the infancy of the Republic to the present day . . . . (60) [Jackson, 2nd inaugural].

> Intelligence, patriotism, Christianity, and a firm reliance on Him who has never yet forsaken this favored land are still competent to adjust our present difficulty. (126) [Lincoln, 1st inaugural].

> I must utter my belief in the divine inspiration of the founding fathers. Surely there must have been God's intent in the making of this new world Republic. (207) [Harding].

The central idea of the public philosophy as expounded in the inaugural address is neither liberty nor equality but "the Nation" (always capitalized). Indeed, the main theme of the early presidential addresses was the preservation, still feared to be problematic, of the Union. Thomas Jefferson could with his customary urbanity declare that

If there be any among us who would wish to dissolve this Union or to change its republican form, let them stand undisturbed as monuments of the safety with which error of opinion may be tolerated where reason is left free to combat it. (14) [1st inaugural].

Successive presidents, on the other hand, with mounting concern as the time approached for the fateful "War Between the States," as the Civil War was called in the South, called for the "preservation of the . . . integrity of the Union" and of its "General Government" against fissiparous tendencies in the states. The states, declared Andrew Jackson, must

indignantly frown . . . upon the first dawning of any attempt to alienate any portion of our country from the rest or to enfeeble the sacred ties which now link together the various parts. (59) [2nd inaugural].

In 1841 William Henry Harrison could complain that "there exists in the land a spirit . . . hostile to liberty itself. . . . It looks to the aggrandizement of a few even to the destruction of the interests of the whole." Speaking direly "from this high place" of the dissolution of the Roman republic, Harrison intoned that "in the Roman Senate Octavius had a party and Anthony had a party, but the Commonwealth had none." Then came his rhetorical climax:

It is union that we want, not of a party for the sake of a party, but a union of the whole country for the sake of the whole country. (86, 87)

James K. Polk repeated the oftsounded inaugural theme that, after the tumult and the shouting dies, the President, even though head of his party, "should not be president of a part only, but of the whole people of the United States." (98)

The theme that the Nation is much more than a Lockeian calculation of interests was sounded by Franklin Pierce in 1853 and James Buchanan in 1857:

With the Union my best and dearest earthly hope are entwined. Without it what are we individually or collectively? [Pierce, 108.].

It is an evil omen of the times that men have undertaken to calculate the mere material value of Union. [Buchanan, 113].

Finally, the crescendo of concern for the preservation of the Nation reaches its climax in the poignant imagery of Abraham Lincoln:

The mystic chords of memory, stretching from every battlefield and patriot grave to every living heart and hearthstone all over this broad land, will yet swell the chorus of Union, when again touched, as surely they will be, by the better angels of our nature. [1st inaugural, 126].

It was not until William McKinley's 1897 address that the danger of a breakup of the Union could be declared finally and definitely put to rest. "The North and South," he said, "no longer divide on the old lines but upon questions of principles and policies; and in this fact surely every lover of the country can find cause for true felicitation." (176)

With Theodore Roosevelt there commences an evocation of the Nation as the center of the American public philosophy with a different accent. No longer is the concern a negative one: to prevent the breakup of the Union and to see that within the federal system prescribed by the Constitution the states give due acknowledgement of the role of the "General Government." Now there commences talk of dramatic changes in social and economic conditions requiring a more active role for the national government than in the past. This shift toward an "activist" concept of the Nation is sometimes said to have been the responsibility of the modern Democratic presidents (plus the maverick Theodore Roosevelt). Judging by the inaugural address, however, the shift toward an activist understanding of the Nation as the centerpiece of the public philosophy is bipartisan.

The idea that "tremendous changes" had occurred in American society as a result of "modern life" was the *Leitmotif* of Theodore Roosevelt's address in 1905:

Our forefathers faced certain perils which we have outgrown. We now face other perils, the very existence of which it was impossible that they should foresee. Modern life is both complex and intense, and the tremendous changes wrought by the extraordinary industrial development of the last half century are felt in every fiber of our social and political being. (184).

Roosevelt's more conservative successor, William Howard Taft, offered essentially the same analysis in his speech of 1909:

The scope of modern government in what it can and ought to accomplish for its people has been widened far beyond the principles laid down by the old 'laissez faire' school of political writers, and this widening has met popular approval. (189).

It was in the rhetoric of Woodrow Wilson's first inaugural that the new activist interpretation of the idea of the Nation took on definitive form. Contending that his election meant much more than a change in party, Wilson continued

The success of a party means little except when the Nation is using that party for a large and definite purpose. (199)

Gaining eloquence and waxing lyrical as he proceeded, Wilson declared that
> This is the high enterprise of the new day: to lift everything that concerns our life as a Nation to the light that shines from the hearthfire of every man's conscience and vision of the right. (202)

He concludes with a call to national reformation and renewal. Such a reformation, he declares passionately,
> will be no cool process of mere science. The *Nation has been deeply stirred* . . . The feelings with which we face this new age of right and opportunity sweep across our heartstrings like some air out of God's own presence, where justice and mercy are reconciled *and judge and the brother are one.* [Emphasis added.] (202)

The lyrical tone of Wilson's address, which today would be too "hot" to convey over the tube (as Marshall McCluhan would say), should be carefully attended to as one of the most important expressions of the American public philosophy as expressed by presidents. The assumption should be made that "reasonable persons" of the times responded to Wilson's eloquence as a splendid example of the "rhetoric of assent." Wilson's assertions that the American Nation has a will; that presidential elections, however closely divided, are often the indications of a dramatic new phase in the unfolding of that will; and that the presidency is more than a merely "political" office but is a kind of "secular Pope" to use Antonio Gramsci's phrase, through which the public philosophy is interpreted and if need be revised, were accepted as "warrantable assertions" by "men of goodwill." Thus, whatever we might think of it in terms of the "cool" style prevalent today, for the audience he sought to move, Wilson's peroration was unquestionably effective:

> We know our task to be no mere task of politics, but a task which will search us through and through, whether we be able to understand our time and the need of our people, whether we indeed be their spokesmen and interpreters, whether we have the pure heart to comprehend and the rectified will to choose our life course of action.
> This is not a day of triumph; it is a day of dedication. Here muster not the forces of party, but the forces of humanity. Men's hearts wait upon us; men's lives hang in the balance; men's hopes call upon us to say what we will do. Who shall live

9

up to the great trust? Who dares fail to try? I summon all patriotic, all forward looking men to my side. God helping me, I will not fail them, if they will but counsel and sustain me! (202) [End of 1st inaugural].

In his second inaugural (1917) Wilson spoke of Americans as having become "citizens of the world."

And yet we are not the less American . . . We shall be more American if we but remain true to the principles in which we have been bred. They are not the principles of a province or a single continent. We have known and boasted all along that they were the principles of a liberated mankind. (204)

The "fires of war" that "blaze throughout the world," were forging Americans into "a new unity." (205)

After the allied victory, Wilson, in failing health, lost the battle for American membership in the League of Nations. His successor claimed that his victory over the Democratic candidate was a triumph of "nationality" over "internationality.":

The success of our popular government rests wholly upon the correct interpretation of the deliberate, intelligent, dependable popular will of America. In a deliberate questioning of a suggested change of national policy, where internationality was to supersede nationality, we turned to a referendum, to the American people. (209).

Despite their dramatic differences, the idea of the public philosophy as the result of the Nation's "will' is as central a theme to Harding's rhetoric as it had been to Wilson's. A careful study might show that the difference between Wilson's insistence upon the United States' joining the world and Harding's invitation for the world to join the United States were variations on a theme rather than opposing positions. "When the Governments of the world shall have established a freedom like our own," Harding declared, "war will have disappeared." (210, 213)

Calvin Coolidge's 1925 inaugural contains numerous passages that read as if they could have been written by Woodrow Wilson himself. What Harding had with disapproval referred to as the policy of "internationalism" seems again to have come into vogue with the man who had been Harding's Vice-President:

. . . we cannot live unto ourselves alone . . . (215)

tion. They have asked me to be the present instrument of their wishes. In the spirit of the gift I take it.

In this dedication of a Nation we humbly ask the blessing of God. May He guide me in the days to come. (End) (239)

Unless they are seen in the context of the American public philosophy and the centrality accorded by it to the idea of the Nation, is it possible to interpret aright the terms "mandate," "instrument" and the like? The Nation that is being celebrated is, of course, that founded on the principle of limited government. It is a Nation *of diverse individuals* that is being defended and promoted. As Roosevelt said in his Second Inaugural:

Today we reconsecrate our country to long-cherished ideals in a suddenly changed civilization . . . . *In our personal ambitions we are individualists.* But . . . in our seeking for economic and political progress *as a nation*, we all go up, or else we all go down, as one people. (243, emphasis added)

Using the rhetoric of assent, President Roosevelt devoted almost the entirety of his third inaugural to the theme of the Nation. "On each national day of inauguration," he began, "the people have renewed their sense of dedication to the United States." This time he referred to the "spirit" of America:

. . . if the spirit of America were killed, even though the Nation's body and mind, constricted in an alien world, lived on, the America we know would have perished. That spirit—that faith—speaks to us in our daily lives in ways often unnoticed . . . . It speaks to us here in the Capitol of the Nation. It speaks through the process of governing in the sovereignties of the 48 States . . . . (246)

The President, speaking in a moment of the greatest danger for liberty, quoted Washington's first inaugural in 1789:

The preservation of the sacred fire of liberty and the destiny of the republican model of government are justly considered deeply, finally, staked on the experiment entrusted to the hands of the American people. (246)

The physical configuration of the earth has separated us from all of the Old World, but the common brotherhood of man, the highest law of our being, has united us by inseparable bonds with all humanity. (217)

What might be called the American public philosophy of theocentric, non-apocalyptic exceptionalism was given an expression exaggerated even for the lyricism appropriate to inaugural addresses in the following words of the usually cool Coolidge:

America seeks no earthly empire built on blood or force. No ambition, no temptation, lures her to thought of foreign dominations. The legions which she sends forth are armed, not with the sword, but with the cross. The higher state to which she seeks the allegiance of all mankind is not of human, but of divine origin. She cherishes no purpose save to merit the favor of Almighty God. (223)

Coolidge's concluding paragraph is remarkable in many respects, not the least of which is its presumption of American innocence in an otherwise wicked world. To seize upon it simply as an example of hyperbole, however, would be to miss its significance as an excellent illustration of the American public philosophy. In particular, one should not yield to the temptation to confuse the American idea of the Nation with "nationalism" as a messianic ideology of the type espoused by Fichte or Mazzini in the nineteenth century or by "national liberation movements" in the twentieth. Whereas the former celebrates multiethnicity (as, for example, President Ford's felicitous comparison in his Bicentennial Address on July 5, 1976 at Monticello, of America to Joseph's coat of many colors), the latter typically arises from the claim on behalf of a single ethnic group for political independence. A second distinction between the American concept of the Nation and the "national liberation movements" today is that the latter are typically tied to a style of politics compatible with collectivism and the single party as the expression of that collectivity's "will." Even where Woodrow Wilson used rhetoric that taken out of context sounds like Rousseau and the "general will," in the context of the American public philosophy, his words take on a different hue.

Indeed, if Wilson is a nationalist of the political messianic kind —and here one recalls the classic study by J.L. Talmon—so was Coolidge when he called on Americans to be more national and less sectional in their thought. (223) And it is difficult to see how Wilson, the alleged "internationalist," could qualify as a messianic nationalist.

Even if apocalyptic rhetoric has been employed at times; and even if such rhetoric (as Robert Bellah has shown in *The Broken Covenant)* has been present in the cultural atmosphere from the beginning of American history (the Puritans, Tom Paine, etc.), the fact remains that the United States *has* been "exceptional" among the world's peoples in the circumstances of its beginning. As a "new" nation, the United States lacked a culture extending back over the centuries—or even millennia—in the past which could give it a *mission civilisatrice.* What America needed above all was to be let alone by the European powers. Given that the idea of a national collective "will" so central to political messianism clashed directly with the American exaltation of the private individual, and given the American aversion to militarism and dictatorship, it is inappropriate to look at American political life through the lenses of concepts appropriate to Europe following the French revolution. In the American public philosophy, the United States is a nation *under* God, not a collectivity *equivalent* to the divine will. The American *novus ordo seclorum* or "New Order for the Ages," was just that—a fresh, novel, unexpected event, but an event which took place within pragmatic history. The Puritan idea of founding the Kingdom of God on earth was rather far removed from the mind of the author of the *Declaration of Independence.* Thomas Jefferson could not have disagreed more with the words of the seventeenth-century English political theorist and martyr to the cause of Puritan republicanism, James Harrington, who had written that it was the duty of a "free commonwealth" to be "a minister of God upon earth, to the intent that the whole world be governed with righteousness."[15] Lest one be given to exaggerate the influence of apocalyptic rhetoric from the Books of *Daniel* and *Revelation* on the American political consciousness, one need only recall that Jefferson was the author of the Virginia Statute for Religious Freedom and that James Madison authored *Federalist Number Ten.*

It is in the light of the American public philosophy of the Nation that Franklin D. Roosevelt's rhetoric deserves to be examined. In a recent article on President Reagan's "New Federalism," Samuel H. Beer takes issue with Reagan's oft-repeated assertion that it was the states that created the federal government and not the reverse. The real source, Beer contends, was "the people in collectivity." Turning to Roosevelt's famous first inaugural, Beer correctly indicates that "No other thematic term faintly rivals the term 'nation' . . . in emphasis" in the address.

Coming at the depths of the Great Depression, FDR's first inaugural was one of the greatest expressions of the American public

philosophy ever penned. Through it, Roosevelt showed h(ident, through speech, is uniquely in a position to offer h times by fostering in the ordinary citizen a sense of equa tion in the drama of the Nation's history.

The first line of the speech sets its tone:

This is a day of national consecration. (Schlesinger, I,7)

Then he proclaims his great words of hope (possibly ta Seneca):

This great Nation will endure as it has endured, will reviv will prosper. So, first of all, let me assert my firm belief th only thing we have to fear is fear itself . . .

In Roosevelt's 1933 inaugural, the Nation is spoken of as a "t from which "the money-changers have been driven." The tas administration is said to be to "restore that temple to the a truths." (236) What are the ancient truths? Those of the Christian ethic:

Happiness lies not in the mere possession of money; it lies the joy of achievement, in the truth of creative effort.

Our true destiny is not to be ministered unto but to minister.

It is false to assume that material wealth is the standard (success. (236)

Recalling the Nation from what de Tocqueville had termed a fa "individualism," the President continued: "Restoration calls not a change in ethics alone. This Nation asks for action, and acti now." (237) After citing some examples of the programs he means undertake to combat the Depression, Roosevelt ends his first ina gural with an evocation of the American idea of the Nation as th core of the American public philosophy:

We face the arduous days before us in the warm courage of the national unity; with the clear consciousness of seeking old and precious moral values; with the clear satisfaction that comes from the stern performance of duty by old and young alike. *We aim at the assurance of a rounded and permanent national life.* [Emphasis added].

We do not distrust the future of essential democracy. The people of the United States have not failed. In their need they have registered a mandate that they want direct, vigorous ac-

III. FROM THE NATION TO THE SUPERNATION: THE COLD WAR

Thus far, I have argued that there is a special type of public speech—expressed paradigmatically in presidential inaugural addresses—which articulates the "public philosophy" around which the American polity is organized. The central idea of this public philosophy is "The Nation," conceived of as a people committed to a set of propositions (first expressed in the *Declaration of Independence*) or "self-evident" truths. I have also argued that despite certain superficial similarities, it would be wrong to classify the American idea of the Nation as a form of "political messianism" or apocalyptic "nationalism." Apocalyptic national doctrines (such as those of Fichte in Germany or Mazzini in Italy) call for the transformation of the world by the "redeemer" nation into a perfect realm, devoid of correspondence with the pragmatic world of everyday existence.

The American public philosophy is *sui generis* and needs to be interpreted in relation to the unique context of American history. While it is hardly a mirror image of pragmatic political reality, the American public philosophy is anchored in that reality. That is to say: There really was something "exceptional" about the beginnings of America, and this exceptional feature lay precisely in the fact that the United States was struck off all at once on the basis of the colonists' affirmation of the "self-evident" principle that "all men are created equal" and are endowed by God with certain "unalienable rights." The rhetoric of the public philosophy has been a rhetoric of hope or assent, as when it was reaffirmed by Lincoln in the midst of the Civil War or by Roosevelt in the throes of the Great Depression.

Although the American public philosophy is not a collectivist ideology and although it does not claim that America has a mission to conquer the world in the name of a new total ersatz-religious truth, that philosophy does make universal claims. Those claims periodically require prudent reinterpretation if the public philosophy is not to slide over into a form of political messianism. So long as the United States was a relatively weak nation and so long as it could count on its geographical isolation to protect it from conquest and the threat of same, the universalism in the *Declaration of Independence* (which reads, after all, that *all* men are created equal) could take the form of America's appearing as model or salutary example for less fortunate peoples to emulate insofar as possible. As American power grew and its commerce expanded, however, the spiritual universalism of the American public philosophy—a universalism which at the same time grew out of the particular, unique American experience of founding—threatened to transform itself into an ideology of the ecumenic type.[18]

In the nineteenth century the desire for territorial expansion—commonly known as "imperialism'—was satisfied through what John O'Sullivan, editor of the *Democratic Review of New York* first called "manifest destiny." It was America's destiny—so obvious as to be "manifest" to everyone—to "over-spread the continent allotted by Providence for the free development of our yearly multiplying millions," O'Sullivan declared in July, 1845 with reference to the annexation of Texas.[19]

It is significant that the phrase "manifest destiny," does not appear in presidential inaugural addresses, whose rhetoric, restrained by the public philosophy, was more sober than that of some enthusiasts for the expansion of American territory into Puerto Rico and the Philippines at the turn of the century. Nor is the racism of a Josaiah Strong or a Senator Beveridge, both of whom called for the "Anglo-Saxonization of mankind" evident in the inaugurals. Such a doctrine of innate racial or cultural superiority for Anglo-Saxons clearly violated the American public philosophy's committment to the equality of all human beings.[20]

Nonetheless, one finds in McKinley's Second Inaugural an ominous claim to have established the compatibility of the expansion of American soverignty to other parts of the world with the public philosophy of the founders:

> The American people, entrenched in freedom at home, take
> their love for it with them wherever they go, and they reject as
> mistaken and unworthy the doctrine that we lose our liberties
> by securing enduring foundations for the liberties of others.
> Our institutions will not deteriorate by extension and our sense
> of justice will not abate under tropic suns in distant seas. (180)

McKinley ignored the fact that in the Philippines there had already existed an indigenous political force capable of ruling the Philippines in freedom for itself. The "rebels," as they were denominated, were the effective representatives of the people of the Philippines at the conclusion of the Spanish-American War. Onofre D. Corpuz, the Philippines' leading political scientist, has described the process in which, ironically, the United States used its superior military power to crush the indigenous Filipino government, itself modelled after its own interpretation of liberal democratic theory, as follows:

> The Philippine Revolution started in mid-1896. Leadership

passed shortly . . . to Emilio Aguinaldo. On October 31, 1896, he issued two manifestoes, both addressed "To the Filipino People." This mode of address was significant. Before this time natives were known separately according to their dialect or to their province or region . . . . Collectively they were called by the Spaniards 'Indios,' after the old and mistaken belief that Magellan had discovered India. Now, however, there was a name for all of them—there was a Filipino nation.

. . . On June 12, 1898 Aguinaldo proclaimed the independence of the Philippines, An appeal for recognition by the foreign powers was issued the same month . . . . A constitutional congress met in September and drafted the first republican constitution of Asia. The Revolution now had a government, a constitution, a united people, and a national leader. The Philippine Republic was proclaimed on January 21, 1899.

But the Republic was not to survive, for it was launched in the shadow . . . of the United States' adventure in imperialism. War with Spain having been declared, a U.S. force sailed out of . . . Hong Kong on April 27, 1898, and destroyed the Spanish navy . . . five days later; the Spaniards . . . delivered Manila to the Americans in August. It was no matter that the Filipinos were in control of their country—except Manila, which was under the Americans—at the time. In December the Spaniards and the Americans agreed by treaty on the transfer of the Philippines to U.S. sovereignty. Conflict between the Filipinos and the Americans was now unavoidable, and hostilities broke out less than a month after the Republic was proclaimed. The issue was never in doubt. President Aguinaldo was captured in 1901, and the ensuing guerrilla resistance ended the next year.[21]

In his 1901 Inaugural, however, President McKinley presented matters differently. "We are not waging war against the inhabitants [note his choice of noun here—inhabitants, not citizens] of the Philippine Islands [not "The Philippines," as the Malolos Constitution had proclaimed their territory to be]. A portion of them are making war against the United States." (182) The mockery of the American public philosophy made by McKinley's address, when Americans were asked to believe that by supporting a new nation's war for independence the United States was enlarging "the bounds of freedom" (McKinley, 180) was not lost on many Americans. Resistance to the colonization of the Philippines was widespread in the United States, producing a veritable *"crise de la conscience américaine,"* as an observer put it.[22]

In his Second Inaugural, McKinley defended the conquest of the Philippines on two grounds. One was paternalistic (the Filipinos were allegedly not "ready" for self-government),[23] and the other, in a curious way, was egalitarian (the United States had proved itself the "equal" of any of the world's great powers by taking and keeping colonies). As he put the matter:

> Surely after 125 years of achievement for mankind we will not now surrender our equality with other powers on matters fundamental and essential to nationality. With no such purpose was the nation created. In no such spirit has it developed its full and independent sovereignty. We adhere to the principle of equality among outselves, and by no act of ours will we assign to ourselves a subordinate rank in the family of nations. (180)

While the easy response would be to dwell on the hypocrisy of the attempt to conceal the fact of conquest under the banner of extending "freedom," further reflection suggests that something else is at work here besides, and/or in addition to hypocrisy. McKinley's remarkable rhetoric attests to the power of the hold which the American public philosophy had upon him. Thus, even McKinley, with his condescension toward the Filipinos, felt called upon to promise "to afford the inhabitants of the islands self-government" as soon as they are "ready" for it. (182) The effect of the public philosophy was to moderate an otherwise unadulterated imperialism and helped ultimately (1946) to result in the peaceful accession of independence to the Philippines by the United States. The United States claimed that its colonization was no more than a temporary measure (perhaps to keep other foreign powers from filling a vacuum that might have been created by a weak Filipino regime) and to its credit steadily moved to increase effective participation in the exercise of power by the Filipinos.

The Philippine experiment foreshadowed the difficulty presenting the American nation as it emerged as a "superpower" after World War II. No longer could it afford the luxury of believing that it might live unto itself. There was no alternative for it but increasingly to "entangle" itself in the web of relationships binding other nations. The result was that the public philosophy—which emphasizes that America is a "beacon" in an at best shadowy world, and precisely for that reason does not wish to immerse itself in the conflicts of that world but to remain an exceptional place, where liberty and equality reign—was threatened in an unprecedented fashion. Woodrow Wilson had been the first president systematically to call upon the American people actively to lead a "crusade" (as distinct from simply standing out as a model) for all the world's peoples to have a republican form of government.[24] Wilson's opponents, conventionally called "isolationists," had in the end prevailed, however, and the United States had remained outside of the League of Nations.

In 1817, Thomas Jefferson had declared that America's role in the world was to "consecrate a sanctuary for those whom the misrule of Europe may compel to seek happiness in other climes." "This refuge once known," he declared, "will produce happiness even of those who remain there, by warning their taskmasters that . . . another Canaan is open where their subjects will be received as brothers . . ."[25] With the expansion of American power and the necessity to ally itself with other nations, including Stalinist Russia, against Nazi Germany and Japan in World War II, the United States could no longer remain a "sanctuary" or "new Canaan," separated by the oceans from the Old World's "misrule." Rather, it had the difficult task of entering into the "muck" of world politics as a superpower (especially in virtue of its possession of the atomic bomb) without at the same time losing its public philosophy of non-apocalyptic exceptionalism.

In the rhetoric of post-World War II presidents one detects a tension between allegiance to the original idea of the (exceptionately fortunate) Nation—a sanctuary in the world jungle, as it were—and to a new idea of America as the Supernation which will save the world. While it could be argued that suggestions of the Supernation idea were present all along in the American public philosophy[26] my thesis is that there is a decisive break in the continuity of the American public philosophy, around the end of World War II, when America began to promise what it could not deliver and when moral aspirations sensible in the American context, and with proper philosophical clarification and elaboration, for any context, became intertwined with pragmatic power considerations to the detriment of both. At the same time, the resilience of the older (more sober, at least as regards expectations for transforming the world) public philosophy tradition was such that it was constantly reasserting itself in an attempt to correct any imbalance in the direction of a hyperactivist Supernation idea. Let us now turn to the evidence.

The Allied victory over Nazi Germany left the United States facing another totalitarian dictatorship in Stalinist Russia. It is scarcely surprising, therefore, to find Harry S. Truman beginning his inaugural on January 20 with a reaffirmation of "the essential principles of the faith by which we live."

> The American people stand firm in the faith which has inspired this Nation from the beginning. We believe that all men have the right to freedom of thought and expression. We believe that all men are created equal because they are created in the image of God. From this faith we will not be moved. (252)

Against this American "faith," there was arrayed the "false philosophy" of Communism. Few sophisticated students of Marxism would recognize the portrait painted of Communism in President Truman's inaugural. From today's vantage point it helps one understand how Senator Joseph McCarthy came to enjoy a temporary success. There has always been the danger in "Americanism" that it might degenerate into a primitive conformity not in keeping with its extolling of the private vision and might adopt a Manichaean view of the outside world.

The climate of opinion today conveyed in the phrase the "cold war" is very much present in Truman's address.[27] The call to "strengthen the freedom-loving nations against aggression" (254) issued at a time when the United States still possessed a monopoly of atomic weapons, was a portent of things to come. Instead of presenting the issue concretely as one of containing the Stalinist dictatorship, President Truman declared America to be launched on a crusade to export its institutions and technology upon what was presumed to be an eagerly waiting mankind. A center of this redemptive mission was American technology. The famous "Point Four" of Truman's address read as follows:

> Four. We must embark on a bold new program for making the benefits of our scientific advances and industrial progress available for the improvement and growth of underdeveloped areas. (254)

President Truman's Inaugural emphasizes that along with alleviating poverty, hunger, and disease, the export of American industrial and scientific technology was indirectly to bring huge rewards to American commerce. (255) Taking the place of the "old imperialism" there was to arise what unimpressed foreign observers were to call the new imperialism of "Americanization." Earlier inaugural addresses had emphasized the exceptional, unique character of the

American experiment. Now the Nation, although still present, seemed to take second place in Truman's inaugural to an abstraction called "democracy":

> Democracy alone can supply the vitalizing force to stir the peoples of the world to triumphant action, not only against their human oppressors, but also against their ancient enemies —hunger, misery, and dispair. (256)

And later:
> Events have brought our American democracy to new influence and new responsibilities. They will test our courage, our devotion to duty, and our concept of liberty.

> But I say to all men, what we have achieved in liberty, we will surpass in greater liberty. (256)

And finally:
> With God's help, the future of mankind will be assured in a world of justice, harmony and peace. (256)

The abstract utopianism of Truman's inaugural, which could be read uncharitably as calling on God to be the incidental helper of American technology, is obviously at variance with the American public philosophy of the Nation. Wilson had spoken of Americans as having become "citizens of the world." (204) Harding had looked forward to the day when "the Governments of the world shall have established a freedom like our own." Neither the one nor the other, however, had anticipated the United States, *by itself*, going out and remaking the entire world in its own image. With the new realities of American power—the catapulting of the Nation to the status of one of two "superpowers" after World War II— serious strains upon the public philosophy developed. Whereas before the American public philosophy was a form of non-apocalyptic exceptionalism, after World War II the rhetoric of inaugurals stressed exceptionalism less, as the new note of the quasi-apocalyptic transformation of the world in a final battle with demonic communism was sounded. The power of common sense latent in the "old" public philosophy helped to prevent an inversion of American beliefs. This common-sense recognition that the American polity itself still had problems aplenty to resolve within its borders and that even its vast military and economic power was limited, helped to restrain the Supernation ideology.

Dwight D. Eisenhower's first inaugural was saturated with the Manichaean imagery of the "cold war." The contrasts between the "light" of the western democracies and the "darkness" of Communism occurs repeatedly.

Of course the public philosophy from its inception had indulged in the light/dark, new/old contrasts, but they had a specificity and an anchorage in reality lacking in the cold war rhetoric. It really was true that from its inception as a Nation, America was different, that it represented a new beginning, and it left behind much of the baggage of past hatreds which had almost destroyed European civilizations. In Eisenhower's address, however, besides the traditional obeissances to "the abiding creed of our fathers" (258) and to the "precepts of our founding documents" (259) there is an abstractly metaphysical reference to "man's long pilgrimage from darkness toward light," (258) and to "freedom" (in the abstract) being "pitted against slavery." (259) The "faith we hold" is said to belong "not to us alone but to the free of all the world." This faith supposedly "binds the grower of rice in Burma and the planter of wheat in Iowa, the shepherd in Southern Italy and the mountaineer in the Andes." (259) While one may grant that President Eisenhower understood well the faith of the farmer of Iowa, it taxes our imaginations to say that he could read the minds of shepherds in Southern Italy and rice planters in Burma. A curious flattening out has occurred in the American public philosophy here. An abstract creed of "freedom" understood as anti-"Communism" has threatened to replace the specific understanding of freedom and equality in the Nation expressed in the earlier versions of the public philosophy.

Turning to Dwight Eisenhower's second inaugural, one notes that an obsession with the cold war has definitely replaced the Nation as its center. The sober exaltation of America as the "heaven-favored land," is transformed into a messianic proclamation: "May the light of freedom, coming to all darkened lands, flame brightly — until at last darkness is no more." (256)

It would be easy to dwell on the quasi-messianic, even gnostic elements of Eisenhower's inaugural addresses.[28] By doing so, however, one would omit the numerous passages expressing the traditional, non-apocalyptic public philosophy. Thus, in his first inaugural, Eisenhower assures America's allies that "we Americans know the difference between world leadership and imperialism." (260) Shortly afterwards he proclaims that :

Honoring the identity and the special heritage of each nation
in the world, we shall never use our strength to try to impress

upon another people our own cherished political and economic institutions. (261)

In the wake of the tragic Vietnam War, it has been easy for some historians to find an "imperialistic" design in the actions and policies of American presidents. To read them in that way is both to indulge in the fallacy of anachronism, and to fail to appreciate the continuing resilience of the public philosophy. It would be more accurate to say that, having become a superpower, the United States was at times proclaimed in presidential rhetoric to be a supernation. But this was only one note in the presidential music. Exaggerated claims were made on behalf of the ability of the United States to influence world developments. At the same time, the United States was arrayed in a very pragmatic sense against the expansion of Soviet power. It became easy to yield to Manichaean temptations (to view one's own side as the repository of all goodness and the other of all evil) when one measures one's own public philosophy based on the dignity of the person against a regime which crushes dissent in its satellites with tanks (Budapest, Prague), and walls in their people (Berlin).

Postwar United States rhetoric and policy, however, have been based neither on apocalyptic, messianic nationalism nor on power-driven imperialism, but rather on a confused (and confusing) attempt to apply the traditional American public philosophy of theocentric, non-apocalyptic exceptionalism to a world which failed to take America for its model. The result has been the arbitrary division of the world into that of the "free" and the "enslaved," even though a majority of the countries with whom the United States has made alliances can scarcely be called "free" in the American public philosophy's understanding of freedom. Instead of being defined in relation to that philosophy, freedom becomes defined as non-Communist. The non Communist nations of the world are the "free" ones in cold war presidential rhetoric. Hence presidential rhetoric concerning foreign policy becomes a mysterious blending of the public philosophy's aspirations with the pragmatic power situation of the post World War II world.

There is one passage in Dwight Eisenhower's second inaugural which in a particularly effective way captures the peculiar blend of the traditional public philosophy of the Nation with the new pragmatic realities:

For one truth must rule all we think and all we do. No people can live to itself alone. The unity of all who dwell in freedom is their only sure defense . . . . No nation can longer be a fortress, lone and strong and safe. And any people, seeking such shelter for themselves, can now build only their own prison. (265)

The key words in the passage are "The unity of all who dwell in freedom is their only sure defense." "Freedom" is here defined as *free from* Communism." A nation is "free" not if it shares the aspirations of the American public philosophy (although such sharing would be preferable, of course) but whether it is free from Communist (here undifferentiated as to whether it be Soviet, Chinese, or indigenous) domination. Here, on January 21, 1957, President Eisenhower articulated a version of the American public philosophy that would lead the country into the disastrous Vietnam War. Going far beyond the principle that the United States could not live unto itself alone—a principle which the American public philosophy had never denied—Eisenhower pronounced the American nation to be part of something called the "unity of all who dwell in freedom." In behalf of this abstract "unity" which is said to be America's "only sure defense," the United States later committed itself to intervening in behalf of South Vietnam.

The United States, it should be noted, was not said to be simply a part of that alleged "unity of all who dwell in freedom." Rather as the superpower, now become the Supernation, it assumed the responsibility for the wellbeing of that "unity." As the "leader of the free world" it could not stand idly by whenever or wherever the world unity of the free was threatened. The implications of such a premise for defense expenditures and for all of American life are obvious. It is also obvious how serious are the strains put upon the American public philosophy of the Nation by the new idea of the Supernation.

John F. Kennedy's inaugural continues the trend toward abstract supernationalism in the postwar inaugural addresses. Although proclaiming himself and his associates "heirs of that first [American] revolution," Kennedy no longer extols the uniqueness of America but flattens out the Jeffersonian "unalienable rights" into general "human rights," which America is pledged to protect "around the world":

Let the word go forth . . . that the torch has been passed to a new generation of Americans . . . unwilling to witness or permit the slow undoing of those human rights to which this Nation has always been committed and to which we are committed today at home and around the world. (267)

24

Here the President makes it sound almost as if all the world is America, and that the task of the American Nation is to prevent the "undoing" of the extensions of itself around the world. There follow the by now familiar pledges to "pay any price, bear any burden, meet any hardship, support any friend, oppose any foe, in order to insure the survival and success of liberty." (268) It was not until much later, with the defeat of American forces in Vietnam, that the unwisdom of these words was manifest to most observers. The older public philosophy took for granted that "liberty" in the rest of the world was something to be won, if at all, in the course of history by the peoples themselves. Most of the world was recognized to be lacking in liberty. With the expansion of Soviet power after World War II, however, a new theme is sounded. Regimes formerly seen as unfree in terms of the American public philosophy (military dictatorships and feudal autocracies) now become bastions of "liberty" if they appear to be threatened by Soviet expansion.

The rhetoric of the United States as the Supernation in charge of promoting "liberty" throughout a world menaced by the powers of darkness (world Communism) would have to be classified as apocalyptic extremism but for the very real threat to world peace of a Soviet dictatorship armed with atomic weapons. For all the grandiosity of Kennedy's rhetoric in proclaiming that

> In the long history of the world, only a few generations have been granted the role of defending freedom in its hour of maximum danger . . . . (269)

the Cuban missile crisis of 1962 made those words look, if not reasonable, at least credible. The unprecedented international political reality of the "balance of terror" did indeed mean that the peace of the world was in "maximum danger." What the Kennedy administration was called upon to defend was not some abstraction called "freedom," however, but the survival of the Nation and the peace of the world.

In his major speech at American University on June 10, 1963, however, John F. Kennedy called for a reexamination of "our attitude toward the cold war."[29] Eisenhower's "crusade for freedom" intended to sweep away the offending Communist forces of darkness. In the American University address, on the other hand, Kennedy is concerned with a tolerance that could insure survival:

> No government or social system is so evil that its people must be considered as lacking in virtue.[30]

In place of the grandiose language of Kennedy's inaugural, one finds in the American University speech a sober reminder of the

limits of the human condition:
> [W]e all inhabit this small planet. We all breathe the same air. We all cherish our children's future. And we are all mortal.[31]

President Kennedy's reminder of our common mortality proved to be chillingly relevant, when he was murdered in Dallas, a thousand days after his inauguration. It will never be known whether he would have halted American military involvement in South Vietnam in time to prevent the debacle there. What is beyond debate is that such involvement was consistent with the assumptions of his promise that Americans would "pay any price, bear any burden, meet any hardship, support any friend, oppose any foe, in order to insure the survival and success of liberty." (268)

In emphasizing the "supernational" theme in postwar presidential rhetoric, I do not in any way intend to imply that the traditional public philosophy was missing. Especially in the area of extending and promoting the civil liberties of black Americans, President Kennedy evoked the public philosophy of the Nation. Thus, in his speech of June 11, 1963, he insisted that

> It ought to be possible . . . for every American to enjoy the privileges of being American without regard to his race or his color. In short, every American ought to have the right to be treated as he would wish to be treated, as one could wish his children to be treated. But this is not the case.[32]

Indeed, it could be argued that despite his obsession with the Vietnam War, Lyndon Johnson's deepest commitment was to inspire the Nation to make new strides in combatting racial discrimination. As Samuel H. Beer has noted, the American commitment to "create within a liberal, democratic framework a society in which vast numbers of both black and white people live in free and equal intercourse—political, economic, and social," has "never before been attempted by any country at any time."[33]

What is new in the American experiment is not the mere coexistence of black and white people—elsewhere small numbers of either race live in relative peace and security as small minority groups within their respective nations in terms of "separate but equal." It is rather the association between large numbers of black and white people as individuals on the basis of equal citizenship in the Nation that is unique to America.

Regardless of his serious technical deficiencies as a public speaker, President Johnson offered a great example of the "rhetoric of assent" in his speech to the Congress in 1964 following the events in

Selma, Alabama, where black and white people who had been peace-fully demonstrating for the civil rights for all citizens were brutally confronted by Sheriff "Bull" Connor. The President said in part:

> I speak to you tonight for the dignity of man . . . What hap-pened in Selma is part of a larger movement . . . of American Negroes to secure for themselves the full blessings of American life. Their cause must be our cause too. Because it is . . . all of us who must overcome the crippling legacy of bigotry. . . .

At this point in his speech, Johnson, as one observer described it, raised his arms and repeated these words from an old Baptist hymn, now the marching song of the civil rights movement: "And . . . we . . . shall . . . overcome.   At this moment . . . "the whole chamber was on its feet . . . . In the galleries Ne-groes and Whites, some in the rumpled sports shirts of bus rides from the demonstrations . . . wept unabashedly."[34]

Although Lyndon Johnson's call to America to build a "Great Society" is frequently treated with derision today, there can be little doubt as to its effectiveness in persuading the Nation to begin more effectively to undo many of the injustices done to black people. The depth of commitment behind the various measures Johnson pro-posed (the Voting Rights Act, the "War on Poverty," "Affirmative Action," etc.) was in sharp contrast to the cold calculation of how best to keep the social peace that lay behind his successor Richard Nixon's support for an extension of some of the same measures.

When one reads Jimmy Carter's 1977 inaugural address, it is clear that the Nation is again at the center of presidential rhetoric in a way in which it had not been since the days of the cold war and Vietnam. Although some abstract utopian pretensions remain—as in his de-claration that it is America's task to "help shape a just and peace-ful world," (*Weekly Compilation*, p. 87) the emphasis in Carter's address is on "help" rather than on "shape."

The first line of Jimmy Carter's inaugural invokes the Nation:

> For myself and for our Nation, I want to thank my predecessor for all he has done to heal our land. (Carter, *Weekly Compila-tion*, p. 87)

He soon proceeds to rearticulate the American public philosophy:

> Ours was the first society openly to define itself it terms of both spirituality and human liberty. It is that unique self-definition which has given us an exceptional appeal—but it also imposes on us a special obligation to take on those moral duties which, when assumed, seem invariably in our best interests. (88)

And later:
Let our recent mistakes bring a resurgent commitment to the basic principles of our Nation, for we know that if we despise our own government, we have no future. (88)

What are the Nation's "basic principles"? What can they be other than liberty and equality? To quote again from Carter's inaugural address:
We have already found a high degree of personal liberty, and we are now struggling to enhance equality of opportunity. Our commitment to human rights must be absolute, our laws fair, our national beauty preserved; the powerful must not persecute the weak, and human dignity must be enhanced.

We have learned that *more* is not necessarily *better*, that even our great Nation has its recognized limits, and that we can neither answer all questions nor solve all problems. (88)

Calling for a muting of the Kennedyesque trumpet call to global action in defense of "democracy," Carter modestly asserts, in keeping with the long course of the public philosophy:
Our Nation can be strong abroad only if it is strong at home. And we know that the best way to enhance freedom in other lands is to demonstrate here that our democratic system is worthy of emulation.

To be true to ourselves, we must be true to others. We will not behave in foreign places so as to violate our rules and standards here at home, for we know that the trust which our Nation earns is essential to our strength. (W.P., 80)

The sobriety in President Carter's inaugural rhetoric is relative, of course. There is something by nature ecstatic about the "American dream," and yet this ecstasy is a sober one. Nonetheless, the peroration referring to "our belief in an undiminished, ever expanding American dream," (89) is puzzling in the light of the earlier declaration that "more is not better." Perhaps by the "expansion" of the American dream, Carter meant to refer to its *extension* to those citizens presently at the margins of the Nation's plenty.

President Carter's realism and common sense came to the fore in a remarkable way in his so-called "malaise" speech of July 15, 1979. ("Energy and National Goals"). Despite his penchant for burying leading ideas under a mountain of programmatic detail—his speechwriter James Fallows has said that he "seemed to have not one point of view but 50 specific beliefs"[35]—at the heart of this speech the President made what in time is likely to become regarded as an enduring contribution to the continuing articulation of the American public philosophy as it ebbs and flows. Although roundly attacked by journalists and others as a political mistake, Carter's address was a noteworthy rearticulation of the public philosophy.

After describing the background to the speech—of how he cancelled what was to have been just another speech on the energy crisis and invited a number of people more skilled in reflection than are the ordinary counselors of Presidents to Camp David—[36] President Carter launched into his theme, "The Crisis of Confidence":

... I want to talk to you ... about a fundamental threat to American democracy.

I do not mean our political and civil liberties. They will endure. And I do not refer to the outward strength of America, a nation that is at peace tonight everywhere in the world, with unmatched economic power and military might.

The threat is nearly invisible in ordinary ways. It is a crisis in confidence. It is a crisis that strikes at the very heart and soul of our national will. We can see this crisis in the growing doubt about the meaning of our own lives and in the loss of a unity of purpose for our Nation. (Jimmy Carter, *Presidential Documents*, 1237)

Carter proceeds to show the "American dream" as rooted in historical reality:

The confidence that we have always had as a people is not simply some romantic dream ... it is the idea which founded our Nation and has guided our development as a people .... Confidence has defined our course and has served as a link between generations. (*Ibid.*)

Carter's identification of the problem as a crisis of "confidence in the future" enabled him to draw on the resources of the public philosophy and use the rhetoric of assent in an attempt to inspire hope in the people. The fact that the speech was immediately greeted with derision in some quarters does not detract from its importance as a good example of presidential rhetoric in the service of the public philosophy. After all, Lincoln was ridiculed by the press for his alleged failure to rise to the occasion at Gettysburg. The impact on public opinion of presidential speech which articulates the public philosophy may be immediate, as with Lyndon Johnson's response to the events in Selma. Such impact has often been delayed, however, as events must catch up with eloquence. Adlai Stevenson's speeches in his 1952 and 1956 campaigns for the presidency against Eisenhower are still remembered by many who were moved by them as classic expressions of the public philosophy.

In an analysis remarkable for its contrition and humility, Carter inveighed against what Reinhold Niebuhr once called the peculiarly American proclivity for self-congratulation. The public philosophy is not to be confused with mindless repetition of traditional pieties when the reality is far removed from the oratorical cliché. As the President expressed it:

> In a nation that was proud of hard work, strong families, close-knit communities, and our faith in God, too many of us now tend to worship self-indulgence and consumption. Human identity is no longer defined by what one does, but what one owns. But we've discovered that owning things and consuming things does not satisfy our longing for meaning. (*Ibid*, 1237)

Later, President Carter read a litany of the horrors of the recent past:

> We were sure that ours was a nation of the ballot, not the bullet, until the murders of John Kennedy and Robert Kennedy and Martin Luther King, Jr. We were taught that our armies were always invincible and our causes were always just, only to suffer the agony of Vietnam. We respected the Presidency as a place of honor until the shock of Watergate. (1237)

As had Roosevelt before him, Carter spoke of the need to rally behind the ideals of the Nation. He insisted on recalling the public philosophy in order to distinguish between an authentic view of freedom and a "mistaken" one:

> . . . There are two paths to choose. One . . . leads to fragmentation and self-interest. Down that road lies a mistaken idea of freedom, the right to grasp for ourselves some advantage over others . . . .
>
> All traditions of our past, all the lessons of our heritage . . . point to another path, the path of common purpose and the restoration of American values. That path leads to true freedom for our Nation and ourselves.

President Carter's speech of July 15, 1979 was no Gettysburg address. It was too long, and its most important observations were sandwiched between a disjointed account of the more thoughtful advice he had received at his "Crisis of Confidence" conference at Camp David and the inevitable *list* of rather trivial steps on the energy shortage. Nonetheless, he had broken his pragmatic stride long enough to reflect on the decline of the American public philosophy in the politics of his time. From that same public philosophy he had discovered sources of renewal and hope.

We are now too close to the administration of Ronald Reagan to make more than a tentative assessment of how his rhetoric fits in with the articulation and re-expression of the American public philosophy.

There is some cause for concern that Carter's return to a sense of limits in his view of the United States' role in world affairs might be reversed in certain respects by Reagan. The latter's ominously titled "Crusade for Freedom" address delivered to the British Parliament in June, 1982, calling for "supporting democratic development" around the globe through a plan that "will leave Marxism-Leninism on the ash heap of history" raised dangers of a revival of the cold war. (Knowledgeable students of Marxism could have told the President that "Marxism-Leninism" had already done a very good job of throwing itself on the "ash-heap" of history, to judge by the stagnant and bureaucratic societies that today make any pretense to following "Marxism-Leninism.") Reagan's 1983 address to a meeting of Evangelical Christians in which he described the Soviet Union as "an evil empire" has also aroused widespread concern.

The greatest challenge to the persuasive powers of the Presidency today is over the threat of nuclear devastation of the earth. Although President Carter addressed the problem eloquently in his Farewell Address, and although there is growing support in the country for a policy of reduction in and eventual elimination of nuclear weapons, the issue has yet to be integrated into the framework of the public philosophy. There are no present signs that Reagan's Presidency will be responsive to the issue. Indeed, under the Reagan administration there may have been a retrogression, as Pentagon strategists play at their games of 'limited" nuclear war, unmindful that they have lost their foothold on reality. As Kenneth W. Thompson has written in his valuable book, *The President and the Public Philosophy*, many Americans have come to view nuclear war as a "practical alternative" to conventional war, whereas "they ought to recognize that a war between the superpowers would likely incinerate the world." A president, Thompson concludes, "must persuade or force the public to think more realistically about the largely incomprehensible dangers of nuclear warfare." And for this the rhetoric of the public philosophy is needed:

> It will not be enough for future presidents to show restraint [in the threat or use of United States military power]; they must help the public *to understand* why restraint is necessary.[37]

In the concluding part of this study, I wish to show the utility of linking presidential rhetoric and the public philosophy by examining an argument recently advanced about rhetoric and the modern presidency.

IV. HAS THERE BEEN A RISE OF THE "RHETORICAL PRESIDENCY"?

According to one scholar, the early years of the 1960's produced a "bumper crop" of presidential studies, most of which fell under the designation "Hallowed Be Thy Presidency." Subsequently, he notes the pendulum has swung the other way, and the *Leitmotif* of such studies has been "Deliver Us from Presidents."[38]

Today we know so much about the grime and grit of recent presidencies that a return to the "Hallowed Be Thy Presidency" theme is unthinkable. The revelations about Watergate and Vietnam have left deep scars in the public consciousness. Americans have learned fast what they already should have known from Lord Acton and the *Federalist Papers* about the tendency of power to corrupt.

It could be, however, that certain institutions have a way of surviving abuse by their occupants. One thinks of the Papacy, for example. While Jean Bodin's *mot juste* to the effect that "a bad man makes a good king" is true only in the sense in which Nietzsche held that truth inheres only in the exaggerations, it *is* true that a good institution neutralizes the mistakes of even its most cynical and manipulative occupiers. To the extent that some kind of Hegelian theory of history seems to emerge, it is, insofar as I know, purely accidential. If Goethe erred in writing *"Amerika—du hast es besser,"* he would have been right on the mark had he said *"Amerika—du hast es verschieden."*

In today's climate of "Deliver Us From Presidents" it is to be expected that sharp revisions of earlier contentions about the President's role of "Teacher and Preacher in Chief" have been forthcoming. One of the more interesting and important of such studies, by my colleague James Ceaser and others, argues that

> As strange as it may seem to us today, the framers of our Con-
> stitution looked with great suspicion on popular rhetoric.
> Their fear was that mass oratory, whether crudely demogogic
> or highly inspirational, would undermine the rational and en-
> lightened self-interest of the citizenry . . . .

Not surprisingly, given the above conclusion about the intent of the
framers, the authors find that the "modern" presidency commen-
cing with Wilson has violated the spirit, if not the letter, of the Constitution. But let me quote their words:

> . . . [T]he framers discouraged any idea that the president
> should serve as a leader of the people who would stir up mass
> opinion by rhetoric; their conception was rather that of a con-
> stitutional officer who would rely for his authority on the for-
> mal powers granted by the Constitution and on the informal
> authority that would flow from the office's strategic position.

The framers thus created the model for "an essentially non-rhe-
torical regime." Lest one misrepresent their position or obtain a
cheap victory by arguing that any nonrhetorical president would
resemble a mummy, Ceaser and his colleagues base their case on a
distinction between rhetoric that is "popular" and rhetoric that is
"public."

> These limitations on popular rhetoric did not mean, however,
> that presidents were expected to govern in silence. *Ceremonial
> occasions presented* a proper forum for reminding the public
> of the nation's basic principles and communications to Con-
> gress, explicitly provided for by the Constitution, offered a
> mechanism by which the people also could be informed on
> matters of policy. Addressed in the first instance to a body of
> informed representatives, it would *possess a reasoned and
> deliberative character.* And insofar as some in the public
> would read these speeches and state papers, they would impli-
> citly be called to raise their understanding to the level of
> characteristic deliberative speech.

Turning to the inaugural address, the authors contend that
Thomas Jefferson's address in his first inaugural—a model which
lasted until the time of Wilson—was primarily an effort "designed to
instruct the people in, and fortify their attachment to, true republican political principles. Up until Wilson's first inaugural, then, presidents consistently attempted to show how the actions of the new

33

administration would conform to constitutional and republican principles."

Against this tradition Woodrow Wilson gave the Inaugural Address . . . a new theme. Instead of showing how the policies of the incoming administration *reflected the principles of our form of government*, Wilson sought to articulate the unspoken desires of the people by holding out a vision of their fulfillment. Presidential speech, in Wilson's view should articulate what is "in our hearts" and not necessarily what is in our constitution.[39]

Although there is more to Professor Ceaser's subtle and complex argument, enough has been offered to suggest its gist, and it will perhaps be obvious even before I state it what my response will be. If my thesis concerning the presidency and the public philosophy has any validity, it will require the abandonment of the contention that there has been any such sharp break in presidential rhetoric of the kind the authors describe. There being no difference between "the principles of our form of government" and the public philosophy, it is simply not the case that any such violation or abandonment or ignoring of those principles has occurred in presidential rhetoric of the kind which the authors discuss.

What after all are those principles? To quote President Gerald Ford, speaking at Monticello on the occasion of the Nation's Bicentennial:

[The United States is] uniquely a community of values, as distinct fropm a religious community, a geographic community, or an ethnic community. This Nation was founded 200 years ago, not on ancient legends or conquests or physical likeness or language, but on a certain political value which Jefferson's pen so eloquently expressed.

"To be an American," Mr. Ford went on to say," is to subscribe to those principles which the Declaration of Independence proclaims and the Constitution protects . . . ." He then went on to compare America to "the beauty of Joseph's coat" with its "many colors." (1975 - 1976)

It is difficult to see how, given the principles of the American public philosophy and the necessities of modern government in an industrialized society, one should or could avoid a presidency that communicates directly to the people. The Constitution enshrined no particular economic system, and it was William Howard Taft, Wilson's predecessor, who said in his inaugural:

The scope of a modern government in what it can and ought to accomplish for its people has been widened far beyond the principles laid down by the old 'laissez faire' school of political writers, and this widening has met with popular approval. (189)

As Abraham Lincoln said long before Woodrow Wilson, the 'central idea' in our political public opinion, at the beginning was ... the "equality of men." And although it has always submitted patiently to whatever of inequality there seemed to be as a matter of actual necessity, its constant working has been a steady progress towards the practical equality of all men.[40]

The increase of direct "rhetorical" appeals to the people by "modern" presidents is undeniable, but it is explicable by other factors than a novel "doctrine" of the presidency. The impact of rampant, heedless industrialization during the last half of the nineteenth century of the American Nation's commitment to equality was rather shattering, to say the least. Who could with cause deplore as rhetoric in the bad sense Wilson's condemnation of the "human cost" of industrialization:

With riches has come inexcusable waste .... We have been proud of our industrial achievements, but we have not hitherto stopped thoughtfully enough to count the human cost, the cost of lives snuffed out, of energies overtaxed and burdened, the fearful physical and spiritual cost to the men and women and children upon whom the dead weight and burden of it all has fallen pitilessly the years through. (207)

While one can readily grant to the authors of the "Rise of the Rhetorical Presidency" their contention that rhetoric is not the same as governing, rhetoric of the kind found in Wilson's address was used as a prelude to concrete actions to remedy in part the inequities and injustices exposed by the rhetoric itself.

Conclusion

I shall not pretend to have exhausted my subject. Many more topics, such as whether today presidential speechwriting by a team of people who may even select the subjects the President discusses as he shuttles endlessly and witlessly across the indeed very extended republic that is the United States has not trivialized presidential rhetoric almost beyond repair, could be considered. But let me leave you with a semblance of my main contention, to wit: the rhetoric of the American presidency is of a special kind when it is truly presidential in that it cannot be viewed aright without recognizing its link to the American public philosophy. Presidential speech is not just the speech of any political leader who can capture a balcony or a television studio. Because of its anchorage in the public philosophy, American presidential speech has the effect of promoting equality, for it includes and brings all of the citizenry into political life as persons of equal dignity and worth.

Presidential rhetoric can also have the effect of keeping the foreign policy of the United States within the bounds of pragmatic reality without sacrificing the nobility of vision inherent in the traditional American public philosophy. To do this, future presidents will have to evoke the spiritual reality of universal humankind as an open society. The open society idea must be rightly conceived: that is, as something other than the imprinting of the American public philosophy or of even more general ideas of western Democracy on a recalcitrant world. Rather, to the extent that the American public philosophy opens itself out to a sympathetic understanding of political styles different from its own but which at the same time reveal human beings innately to be creatures of dignity and worth, to that extent it will uncover the universality implicit in Thomas Jefferson's words about the "self-evidence" of the truths that "all men" (and not just Americans) are created equal. America will open itself to appropriate the richness of humanity's pre-modern past in the symbolisms of myth, philosophy, revelation, and mysticism. Perhaps America will find its "mission" to be to lead humankind into a postmodern world of openness to all the dimensions of reality, nonmetric as well as metric. This leadership would be of a spiritual nature, however, and it would be entirely consonant with the idea that America serve as model rather than as master, an idea rooted in the traditional American public philosophy itself.

Footnotes

1. Doris Kearns, *LBJ and the American Dream* (New York, Harper and Row, 1976), p. 303.

2. *Ibid*

3. Wayne C. Booth, *Modern Dogma and the Rhetoric of Assent* (University of Notre Dame Press, 1974), xvi.

4. James L. Barber, *Presidential Character*, (Englewood Cliffs, N.J., Prentice Hall, 1972), p. 4.

5. President Carter's speechwriter James Fallows distinguished between two types of presidential rhetoric: One is designed to sway public opinion on a specific issue of the day, while "the second kind of . . . rhetoric is that which will . . . try to explain the directions in which things are going." James Fallows, talk on "Rhetoric and Presidential Leadership," Miller Center Research Project, University of Virginia, March 1, 1979, p. 38. It is the second type which I place in the "public philosophy" category. I am grateful to Kenneth W. Thompson, Director of the Miller Center for Public Affairs, for the opportunity to read this transcript.

6. Booth, *op. cit.*, xiv.

7. Juergen Gebhardt, *Die Krise des Amerikanismus* (Stuttgart: Ernst Klett Verlag, 1976), p. 224.

8. To the best of my knowledge, "public philosophy" is a term originating with the publicist Walter Lippmann in the 1950's. It has come to be used more flexibly in recent years. See Richard Bishirjian, ed., *A Public Philosophy Reader* (New Rochelle, N.Y.: Arlington House Publishers, 1978); William Sullivan, *Reconstructing Public Philosophy* (Berkeley, Cal.: University of California Press, 1982); and Kenneth W. Thompson, *The President and the Public Philosophy* (Baton Rouge: Louisiana State University Press, 1981).

9. Gunnar Myrdal, *An American Dilemma*, (2 Vols., New York: Harper and Brothers, 1944), p. 3.

10. *Ibid.*, p. 6.

11. *Presidential Papers of Jimmy Carter*, I, 1977, 958.

12. *Presidential Papers of Lyndon Baines Johnson*, 1965, I, 72.

13. Myrdal, *op. cit.*, p. 8.

14. Unless otherwise indicated, the source of the quotations from the inaugural addresses is: *Inaugural Addresses of the Presidents of the United States from George Washington 1789 to John F. Kennedy 1961* (Washington, D.C.: U.S., Government Printing Office, 1961). To avoid repetition, page numbers to this volume are in brackets in the text.

15. Quoted in William T. Laprade, *British History for American Students* (New York: Macmillan, 1928), p. 335. Harrington's imperialism is overlooked by those who praise him as a spokesman for "civic humanism." Laprade also quotes a poem published in 1655 by Edmund Waller, who hailed Oliver Cromwell as "the world's protector." This is the same Cromwell who invaded Ireland in 1649, driving tens of thousands of Irish Catholics to exile in Spain.

16. Samuel H. Beer, "The Idea of the Nation," *New Republic* July 19 and 26, 1982), pp. 23 - 29 at 27 - 28.

17. In an as yet unpublished paper, Klaus Vondung has demonstrated the difference between apocalyptic and nonapocalyptic rhetoric. As Vondung points out, the purpose of nonapocalyptic rhetoric—i.e., rhetoric that operates within the structure of everyday political reality—is a "spiritual" one: among other things, it aims to "encourage and console." Apocalyptic rhetoric, on the other hand, interprets the historical situation in which the authors find themselves in an exaggerated way and ends with "extreme abuse of the enemy." When "the apocalyptic interpretation aims back at pragmatic reality with the intention of causing pragmatic action," it becomes "not only mendacious in a moral sense, but may induce and justify criminal acts even to the extent of mass murder and genocide." (p. 18 of paper entitled "The Rhetoric of Apocalypse" delivered to the third annual meeting of the International Seminar

for Philosophy and Political Theory, to be published with the conference proceedings).

18. See my *Political Philosophy and the Open Society* (Baton Rouge, La.: Louisiana State University Press, 1982) for a development of this distinct view between universality and ecomenicity, a theoretical distinction made by Eric Voegelin. An ecumenic empire aims to conquer the inhabited world (or *Ecumene* in Greek). A polity witnessing to a universal truth need not expand at all, because it knows that truth and power are distinct and that in any event universal humankind cannot be an object of conquest.

19. Quoted in Ralph H. Gabriel, ed., *American Values: Continuity and Change* (Westport, Conn.: Greenwood Press, 1974), p. 18.

20. In 1883 Josiah Strong, echoing the doctrine of the survival of the fittest, asked rhetorically "is there any reasonable room for doubt that this [Anglo-Saxon] race . . . is destined to dispossess many weaker races assimilate others and mold the remainder, until . . . it has Anglo-Saxonized mankind?" And Senator Albert J. Beveridge, after returning from the Philippines in January, 1900 proclaimed:

> God has not been preparing the English-speaking and Teutonic peoples for a thousand years for nothing but vain and idle self-contemplation and self-admiration. No. He has made us master organizers of the world to establish system where chaos reigned . . . And of all our race he has marked the American people as His chosen nation to finally lead in the redemption of the world.

Both quotations are from Robert Bellah, *The Broken Covenant: American Civil Religion in Time of Trial* (New York: Seabury Press, 1975), p. 38.

21. Onofre D. Corpuz, *The Philippines* (Englewood Cliffs, New Jersey: Prentice-Hall, 1965), pp. 63 - 64.

22. *Ibid*, p. 65.

23. In 1898 McKinley made his famous statement to the effect that the United States would have to "civilize and Christianize" the Filipinos, forgetting that the great majority had been Roman Catholics under Spanish rule for over three centuries. Leland

D. Baldwin, *The American Quest for the City of God* (Macon, Georgia: Mercer University Press, 1981), p. 233. (It is possible, of course, that McKinley did not consider Catholics to be Christians!)

24.   Upon entering the War in 1916, Wilson declared that all shall know that America "puts human rights above all other rights" and that "her flag is the flag not only of America but of humanity." Quoted in Leland D. Baldwin, *op. cit.,* p. 270.

25.   Quoted in Bellah, *op. cit.,* p. 89.

26.   In a personal communication, Robert Bellah has argued that an "enduring tension" exists between sobriety and apocalypticism in the American public philosophy from the beginning. Rather than there occurring a "shift over time" from nonapocalyptic to apocalyptic modes of expression, both poles are always present and one or the other may predominate at a particular period. (Letter to the author of February 9, 1983) There are two differences between his approach and mine. First, Bellah almost exclusively utilizes rhetoric "below" the level of the presidential inaugurals, which I hold to be the "definitive" expression of the American public philosophy. (Bellah even goes so far in his book as to declare that "there is no orthodox interpreter" of the American public philosophy. "The meaning . . . is left to private interpretation, to the speech of any man . . . who has the power to persuade." *Broken Covenant*, p. 46). Second, I do *not* hold that the transition to the rhetoric of the Supernation necessarily amounts to a transition to apocalyptic rhetoric. Even the most of the rhetoric of America as the Supernation is "sober" by comparison with the apocalyptic nationalism of Fichte, Mazzini, and the rest. The main purpose of the Supernation in post-World War II presidential rhetoric is to *influence*, not to conquer in the physical sense. Other nations were expected to recognize what is universally valid in the American experiment and to apply that knowledge to their local conditions. Insofar as the American founding itself had a universal dimension (it marked the advent of a new era in human history—a *novus ordo seclorum*—and proclaimed the rights of "all men" and not only the colonists), the Supernation idea is linked to the idea of the Nation expressed in most pre-World War II inaugurals. Inso-

far as it approximated the hyperactivist version of the American public philosophy (as expressed, for example, in 1900 by Senator Beveridge who claimed that "the American people" is God's "Chosen nation to finally lead in the redemption of the world," by conquest if necessary), there obviously the Supernation idea deforms the American public philosophy and acquires apocalyptic potential. I wish to thank Professor Bellah for his extensive and extremely helpful comments on an earlier draft of this paper. I have only admiration for his work on the American public philosophy.

27. Already in his acceptance speech at the Democratic National Convention in 1948 Truman had declared that America had "finally stepped into the leadership which Almighty God intended us to assume . . ." Truman also said of the Korean War that "the fate of the world depends, to a very large extent, on what we do." Both quotations are from Edward M. Bevins, *The American Sense of Mission* (New Brunswick, New Jersey: Rutgers University Press, 1957), pp. 9 and 10.

28. One author argues that Eisenhower projected the image of the "New World Soul" in his rhetoric. The president claimed that America's stress on "human spirituality" was "unique among nations." Robert S. Michaelson, *The American Search for Soul* (Baton Rouge, Louisiana: Louisiana State University Press, 1975), p. 10. Gnosticism is an ancient body of ideas, predating Christianity, which some authors argue has resurfaced in other forms in modern messianic movements. The gnostic claims to know the mind of God and to dwell in mind at least in a perfect spiritual kingdom. See Eric Voegelin, *The New Science of Politics* (Chicago: University of Chicago Press, 1952).

29. John F. Kennedy, *Public Papers*, (January 1 - November 22, 1963), p. 462. Along with his inaugural, Kennedy's American University speech is frequently reprinted. A useful collection of presidential speeches, including inaugurals, since 1961 is that edited by Theodore Windt, *Presidential Rhetoric: 1961 - 1980* (Second edition, Toronto: Kendall-Hunt, 1980). This collection includes Kennedy's Berlin and Cuban missile crises speeches as well as the famous "Ich bin ein Berliner" declaration. The American University speech is on pp. 40 - 46.

30. *Ibid.*, p. 461.

31. *Ibid.*, p. 462.

32. Windt, ed., *Presidential Rhetoric*, p. 47. The context was Alabama Governor George Wallace's attempt to block the entrance of the University of Alabama to the few black students who had been enrolled by a federal court order. Inevitably, Kennedy also linked the segregation issue to the international situation: "Today we are committed to a worldwide struggle to promote and protect the rights of all who wish to be free." p. 46.

33. Samuel H. Beer, "The Idea of the Nation," *New Republic* (July 19 and 26, 1982), p. 28.

34. Doris Kearns, *op. cit.*

35. Miller Center Lecture, p. 5, Miller Center Research Project, University of Virginia, March 1, 1979.

36. Professor Robert Bellah, one of those invited to Camp David, thought that the speech did not go nearly far enough. He wanted the President to "take the tough line" and propose a "fundamental reorganization of our society along volunteeristic lines in accordance with our long tradition of democratic process." He came away disillusioned by the meeting. "A Night at Camp David: An Interview with Robert Bellah," *Express: The East Bay's Free Weekly* (Friday, July 27, 1979). I am grateful to Professor Bellah for bringing this interview to my attention.

37. Kenneth W. Thompson, *The President and the Public Philosophy* (Baton Rouge: Louisiana State University Press, 1981), p. 161.

38. William G. Andrews, "The Presidency, Congress, and Constitutional Theory," in A. Wildavsky, ed., *Perspectives on the Presidency* (Boston: Little Brown and Co., 1972).

39. James W. Ceaser, et. al., "The Rise of the Rhetorical Presidency," in Thomas Cronin, ed., *Rethinking the Presidency* (Boston: Little Brown and Co., 1982), pp. 233-251, pp. 237-238, 239. Emphasis added.

40. Quoted in J. Gebhardt, *op. cit.*, p. 186; Lincoln, *Collected Works*, II, 385.

Collection of Presidential Speeches
Cited in Text

I.   *Collection of Inaugural Addresses:*

Inaugural Addresses of the Presidents of the United States from George Washington, 1789, to John F. Kennedy, 1961 (Washington, D.C., United States Government Printing Office, 1961).

II.   *Addresses of President Carter:*

Public Papers of the Presidents of the United States: Jimmy Carter; 1977 (in Two Books). Book I: January 20 to June 24, 1977 (Washington, D.C.: United States Government Printing Office, 1977).

Weekly Compilation of Presidential Documents, V. 13, No. 4, 87 - 89.
(Inaugural Address)

Presidential Documents: Ending Friday, July 20, 1979: "Energy and National Goals." Address to the Nation, July 15, 1979. 1235 - 1241.

III.   *Addresses of President Ford:*

Public Papers of the Presidents of the United States: Gerald R. Ford; (1976 - 1977, in 3 books), Book II (Washington, D.C.: United States Government Printing Office, 1979), pp. 1973 - 1977.

IV.   *Addresses of President Kennedy:*

Public Papers of the Presidents of the United States: John F. Kennedy, (Jan. 1 - Nov. 22, 1963) (Washington, D.C.: United States Government Printing Office, 1964), pp. 459 - 464.

V. *Addresses of President Johnson:*

Public Papers of the Presidents of the United States: Lyndon Baines Johnson, 1964 (Washington, D.C., 1965) *"The American Promise,"* March 15, 1964, p. 281.

Public Papers, 1965 (in Two Books, Washington, D.C., 1966).

VI. *Addresses of President Reagan:*

"A Crusade for Freedom," XLVIII *Vital Speeches,* No. 18 (June 1, 1982), 546 - 550. (To the British Parliament, London, June 8, 1982).

"The Atlantic Alliance: Arms Control and Reduction" in *Ibid.,* 550 - 553. (To the West German Parliament, June 9, 1982.

VII. A valuable collection of speeches of recent presidents may be found in Theodore Windt, ed., *Presidential Rhetoric: 1961 - 1980* 2nd. ed., Dubuque, Iowa: Kendall/Hunt Publishing Company, 1980.